Who I Am: American Scar Stories

Written by
Jenny Cutler Lopez

Photographs by
Tim Acuna and
Holly J. Schumacher

Foreword by
David Mezzapelle

SoLo Publishing
Distributed by Ingram Spark

Photographs by *Tim Acuna* of Acuna Studios, Fairfax, Virginia

Photograph of Amy Tippins by *Holly J. Schumacher* of Holly J. Images, Atlanta, Georgia

Design by *Timothy Jones*

Printed in the U.S.A

Who I am: American Scar Stories

F o r e w o r d

When Jenny Cutler Lopez asked me to write the foreword for her new book, *Who I am: American Scar Stories*, I was honored. Every day I connect with people all over the globe who have scars, both physically and mentally. Over the years, I have learned firsthand that those scars define who they are. The stories behind those scars are inspirational and should be shared with others. The good news is that Jenny has made that happen here, and she does it eloquently by combining the beauty of photography with people's unique narratives. She brings home the reality that these people, and countless others, are human. Their scars reflect their strength and their resilience. They also reflect their wisdom.

Every step we take throughout life serves as the basis of our wisdom. As a matter of fact, wisdom is a gift gained from the past that serves as the foundation of our future. It is a by-product of our successes and failures. And, if you share that wisdom with others, you are helping them on their life's journey as well. The stories in this book are full of wisdom, inspiration, and drive that these people so bravely share to help us on our life's journey.

We endure marks upon our lives every day—some good, some not so good. Think back to a great day when a lasting memory was formed. Think about a successful day at a favorite sport, or receiving that degree you worked for over many years. How about when you met your spouse or significant other? Perhaps the birth of a child has left a lasting mark on you. Conversely, there were some tough moments in your past that probably also left a mark; these negative memories can be hard to shake off.

According to most dictionaries, a scar is defined as "a mark left on something." No matter how you look at the definition, people with scars are still people. They have a brain and a heart. They have meaning and purpose. And, they also have feelings. We should understand, respect, and appreciate people for who they are. Their beauty lies in their human nature and the goodwill they share with others.

This book celebrates people and how every one of us is special, including our special marks. I am confident that you will enjoy it and immediately form a bond with these 12 amazing people Jenny features.

All the Best,

David Mezzapelle

Jupiter, Florida – December 2013
Bestselling Author of *Contagious Optimism* (Viva Editions)

Who I Am: American Scar Stories

Courtney Ott

S t o r y   1

ne summer not long after her operation Courtney wore a swimsuit to a beach on Virginia's coast. Still conscious of her scars, she tried to ignore the strangers staring at her legs. Eventually one woman walked over to ask Courtney how she got her scars. Courtney responded, "Shark bite. Watch out if you go in the water."

Now fifteen and confident, Courtney has blossomed since that day at the beach. She embraces her scars and the story behind them, her journey a remarkable one.

She says, *"My scars show what I have been through. My scars are a part of who I am."*

She exposes her scars whenever she plays basketball or dresses for a high school formal; she wears shorts through the long humid summers in her hometown of Fishersville, a town of 9000 people tucked in Virginia's rural farmlands close to the Blue Ridge Mountains.

But her confidence and wit didn't guarantee her a spot on the high school junior varsity basketball team. The summer before freshman year Courtney trained six days a week for fall tryouts. She practiced her jump shots and ball control. She relearned how to sprint. She lifted weights at the gym four times a week. And when she showed up for tryouts, it signified a victorious end to four years of physical therapy, two years in a wheelchair, and one year recovering from a broken disc in her lower back—all the result of a ten-inch tumor in her left leg.

During the winter of 2008, just before her tenth birthday, Courtney complained her leg hurt. Having raised five other children, her mom Jane chalked up Courtney's pain to run-of-the-mill childhood mishaps until she watched her daughter half-run, half-limp across their yard to catch the school bus. Jane called the pediatrician, who suggested Jane take Courtney to see her husband, an orthopedic surgeon. After X-raying Courtney's leg, the doctor returned to the examination room with tears in his eyes.

Within a week, a biopsy confirmed their worst fears. Courtney began chemotherapy at University of Virginia Hospital. After three months of treatments, Courtney and her parents agonized over the next step: amputation.

Jane says, *"When Courtney was sick, we kept her involved in every decision,"* so together they decided to heed the advice of the only surgeon at Johns Hopkins University who encouraged her to skip amputation and undergo surgery. The surgeon removed the tumor, muscle tissue, nerves, and skin from her right leg and upper left thigh, guaranteeing an arduous and long recovery. But Courtney kept her leg.

The surgery proved to be the first step in a four-year marathon of recovery. But the people of Fishersville wove a web of support around them. Courtney still appreciates what her neighbors, teachers, and friends did for her during the first year of recovery. She says, *"Everyone came forward. No one backed off."*

For the first year, neighbors delivered three meals a week to the house, helping alleviate the stress,

expense, and management of preparing dinners for the family of eight. Jane returned to night shifts at the hospital, her husband went back to his day job, and friends scheduled morning visits to ensure Courtney ate a good breakfast and stayed off her recovering leg. Two daily hour-long dressing changes on Courtney's incisions continued for months and people from their church laundered the dirty bandages. Each day, the handicap bus pulled into the driveway to pick up Courtney for school and the community continued to donate gift cards, toys, and meals to the Ott family, illuminating a generous community protecting one of its flock.

In Fishersville, Courtney is not just the girl who beat cancer. She raced her way to the title of 2010 Super Stock Soap Box Derby Winner for the Blue Ridge region, competing against kids from across America at nationals in Akron, Ohio. She's the voice behind public service announcements. She's a family girl. She's the sibling who labored at physical therapy three times a week until she could walk down the aisle as a bridesmaid at her big sister's wedding. She's the young woman so inspired by the pediatric nurses, spending time with them whenever she visits the hospital for follow-up scans, she wants to become a pediatric nurse after college. And not least of all because of her never-give-up attitude Courtney is now a starter on her high school junior varsity basketball team.

My scars show what I have been through. My scars are a part of who I am.

Courtney Ott

José Rios

l Salvador lost José Rios, a friendly, smart eleven-year-old, at the height of its gang violence and record-high murder rates. José's hometown, La Union, a sluggish coastal town hemmed in by a dreary waterfront and a departure port for nearby Pacific islands, set the stage for his first scar: a small mark dividing his right eyebrow—a result from a fall out of one of La Union's trees.

A year later, scared and speaking only Spanish, José and his grandmother turned their backs on the only life he knew when they arrived in the US to live with family in Texas, followed by a move to his uncle's house in Virginia four years later.

It was in Virginia, fifteen years later and twenty miles west of Washington, DC, where two thugs lingered in a poorly lit parking lot. One clutched a tire iron; the other clutched the wheel of a running car waiting for José.

Earlier that evening, José had decided to go for drinks at Laylas—a bar hidden behind a suburban strip mall. The dance club boasted two dollar pints, three dollar martinis, and a crowded dance floor seven nights a week. Now twenty-six years old, José managed salesmen at a mattress store during the day and spent time with his daughter on the weekends.

Not quite last call, two men approached José. They called him a gangster. José walked toward the exit, continued through the parking lot, when the thug with a tire iron appeared. He struck José across the head, knocking him out. José lay unconscious on the asphalt and the attacker's accomplice slammed his foot on the gas, speeding toward José.

Fate interjected. One of Laylas bouncers stepped outside as the car raced toward José. He shot across the parking lot, pulling José to the sidewalk just as the speeding car made contact with José's face. The friction of the tire flayed the skin from his hairline to his cheekbone, *"peeling it back like a mango,"* says José.

José regained momentary consciousness under the bright lights in the ambulance, passing out again and not waking up until after emergency surgery. His memory of the attack flooded back only after seeing his reflection in the mirror: his face held together with more than eighty staples. The wounds took three months to heal, but the scar will be with José for life.

José's scar serves as a positive reminder of the night that changed his life. *"I'm happy I didn't lose my eye that night,"* he says. Soon after his attack, José switched careers, choosing to help people as a fitness consultant at Gold's Gym. He works hard to ensure his daughter's dream of medical school becomes a reality. He attends church on a regular basis now. *"God is great. My goals are to work hard and go to church,"* he says. And he forgives his attackers, both of whom were caught, charged, and sentenced to twelve years apiece. His dreams of a better life are now bearing fruit after he almost lost everything.

I'm happy I didn't lose my eye that night.

José Rios

BethAnn Telford

e pride ourselves on our independence. And relying on other people proves difficult for most of us, pushing us outside our comfort zone and testing our patience. Diagnosed at thirty-five years old and given two years to live, BethAnn learned she must rely on the people in her life if she wanted to prove her doctors wrong.

Nine years after diagnosis, nine years of relying on her partner Dr. Bob Latin, her mom Suzanne, her dad Bob, her sisters, her extended family members, her friends, and even strangers, BethAnn is now a role model to thousands of people. She raises hundreds of thousands of dollars, nationwide awareness, and a world of *hope* against the brain tumors threatening to kill her and thousands of other Americans.

Her brain tumor causes seizures, blindness, bladder incontinence, and memory loss and her scars mark these trials of the last nine years. When she looks in a mirror, she sees the scar from her bladder augmentation trailing her abdomen and the two scars on her lower back from implanted bladder pacemakers. When she looks in the mirror to brush her waist-long hair extensions, she remembers the scars from two brain surgeries crisscrossing her head. And beneath these outer evidences of her illness are the unseen ones. Her tumor pushes on her left eye leaving her ninety-five percent blind on that side so BethAnn relies on friends to help her train for triathlons, asking them to run and bike on her left side to alert her to any obstacles. Risk of seizures means she relies on hired drivers for her daily commute to the U.S. Government Printing Office.

Frequent interviews by reporters and a non-stop schedule means she relies on Bob to help her with her failing memory.

In BethAnn's first operation, surgeons discovered her brain tumor snaked around a major blood vessel, rendering it inoperable. Post surgery, the surgeon visited BethAnn in her hospital room. He told her she had two to three years to live, and although she may walk again, she most likely would never run. Still in her hospital bed, BethAnn asked for a pen and piece of paper. She wrote a bucket list; a bucket list prodding her onwards for nine years.

Four months after hearing she might never run again, BethAnn ran across the finish line of a 5K race in Harrisburg. Two months later, she completed the Marine Corps Marathon. Two years later, pounding rain and bike crashes were no match for her determination in her first triathlon at Lake Placid.

She's gone toe to toe with the disease, creating TeamBT—a fundraising and awareness-raising organization numbering more than three hundred people. Determination and nation-wide support has encouraged BethAnn to complete the Boston Marathon three times, in addition to twenty-seven other marathons and multiple Eaglemans and Irongirls.

She credits her determination and perseverance to her father. *"He has always been my role model and has taught me to never give up on myself or what I believe in. I have applied this lesson to everything I have done, from school and athletics earlier in my life to fighting my cancer and finding a cure now."*

BethAnn grew up in a working-class home in Harrisburg, Pennsylvania. She attended college and eventually worked with high-ranking officials at the US Capitol and the legislative branch. Extending around her spiral staircase at home are large framed photographs of BethAnn with a number of athletes and politicos, including one of her arm-in-arm with George W. Bush. Another photograph shows her and her cousin Nathaniel, who died of an aggressive stage-IV brain cancer at sixteen years old.

There is a dichotomy to BethAnn; unapologetically determined, she remains soft spoken, relaying confidence without arrogance. She broadcasts her message at fundraisers and award ceremonies across the nation and in countless newspaper articles and sports magazines such as ESPN and Shape. The Discovery Channel featured her in a full-length documentary entitled Silent Suffering.

The last item on her bucket list was also her biggest athletic achievement: the 2012 Kona Ironman World Championship. Over fifteen grueling hours, she swam 2.4 miles, biked 112 miles, and ran 26.2 miles. Refusing to let her blind eye slow her down, BethAnn followed another swimmer, kicking when he kicked. Kona occurred before her bladder surgeries, so BethAnn self-catheterized for the entire race. And as she ran across the finish line, she carried a large white flag over her head, the word Hope written atop many names—the names of children dead from cancer, children fighting cancer, and young survivors of cancer. Removal of BethAnn's pituitary gland during brain surgery left her unable to have children but she embraces the children named on the flag, their anniversaries—the deaths, the clean bills of health—embedded on her heart.

Since this happened to me, my life has changed for the better.

B e t h A n n   T e l f o r d

She says, *"A big part of my determination to help the many children with brain cancer and other cancers is I have had a wonderfully full life, and my heart aches to see a child suffer with this terrible disease."*

For nine years, BethAnn's quiet magnetism and broad smile has helped her raise $450,000 and widespread awareness for the 688,000 Americans living with a brain tumor. Her courage roars back at brain cancer some days, and other days—such as the days when she was learning to walk, or the days her strength wanes, or the weeks she is unable to exercise after another surgery—she tells herself she will try again tomorrow. She says, *"Since this happened to me, my life has changed for the better. I'm a much more giving person now."*

And she does continue to give—by lifting up others diagnosed with brain cancer and sharing her hope by looking them in the eye and telling them to never, never, never give up.

Krystian Leonard

Krystian chose the perfect revenge for her bullies. After five years of schoolyard alienation and ringing taunts, she made a conscious decision. She rejected the negative self image concocted by the kids who pushed her around, ridiculing her scars, labeling her Frankenstein and Ugly. At fourteen, her self-esteem budding, Krystian took a deliberate step. She cultivated a plan—one allowing her to blossom, to draw on her experiences, to broadcast her message of acceptance of physically scarred people. A message she wished she'd heard when she acquired her first noticeable scar as a seven-year-old.

Her first scar resulted from the removal of a benign tumor on her left leg. After the surgery, she returned to second grade at her school in rural West Virginia and experienced bullying for the first time. After a difficult year, her self-esteem wilting, she asked for a scar revision. *"I thought I would never be beautiful,"* she says. *"I thought no one would ever want me."*

The scar revision didn't go as planned. Just before her ninth birthday, Krystian lay on the operating table, waiting for the local anesthetic to take effect, happy she would be rid of the scar she claimed caused the bullying. The doctor began the procedure, but her body reacted negatively to the local anesthetic. Immune to the painkiller, she endured the operation beyond the expected forty-five minutes, the revision extending into a two-hour ordeal. A seven-inch groove remained on her leg, but Krystian promised herself after the procedure she would never ask for a scar revision again.

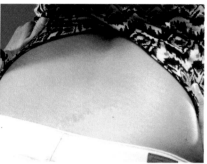

Krystian was back in the operating room the next year, this time for a mutating birthmark on her lower back. Her doctor feared melanoma and removal was imperative. The summer between fifth and sixth grade, while her classmates swam in the local pool and biked around the neighborhood, Krystian slept upright in a chair, unable to lie down or sit in soft seats, including the family car. In the fall, she returned to school, to the familiar alienation, experiencing life as one of the reported fourteen million children bullied each year in the United States.

It took two years after the bullying ended for Krystian to decide it was time to heal and time to love her scars.

She says, *"I looked around and saw how a lot of girls my age thought they needed to be as perfect as a Barbie Doll to be accepted."* And at fourteen, she planted the seeds for her plan. Her first step: she joined the Miss America circuit. She competed in the Miss America Scholarship Organization preliminary pageant and six months later won the title of Miss Southern West Virginia's Outstanding Teen. A year later, she won the title of Miss Northern West Virginia's Outstanding Teen. Her platform: *"Finding strength and building character to redefine self."*

Her plan to share a message of self-acceptance took root in her role as Outstanding Teen, but she works far beyond the requirements of promoting her platform. She launched an organization called Shining S.C.A.R.S, which brings her into local hospitals through the Children's Miracle Network. Krystian visits children and gives them homemade bears. She reads from her first published book, Shining Scars—a story about a struggling star named Eugene learning to overcome stigma and accept his scars.

"I want to help children and teens who are healing from scars to learn to love their bodies just as I have," says Krystian.

She shares her message on radio shows, newspaper articles, magazine features, and on the stage. And in early 2014 she stood on a stage in Florida, sharing her message of self-acceptance and redefining beauty in her Ted Talk, continuing to tell her story to an ever-expanding audience.

I thought I would never be beautiful.

Krystian Leonard

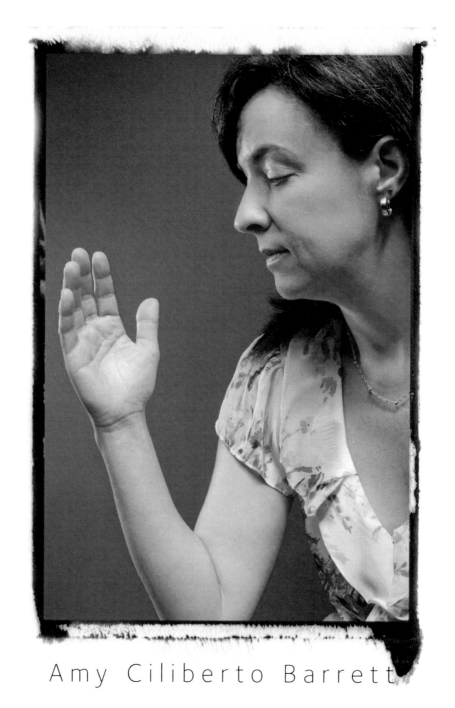

Amy Ciliberto Barrett

S t o r y   5

my grew up in an Italian-American neighborhood forty years ago and has the scars to prove it. In the 1970s, kids across America, shooed outside by their mothers, biked for miles, built camps in old lots, and played pickup games with neighborhood pals. Exploration taught life lessons—life lessons memorialized in stories of broken bones and lifelong scars.

Amy acquired her first scars around the time her parents divorced. At four years old, Amy and her best friend Darlene were playing inside Darlene's garage. They discovered Darlene's older brothers had locked them inside. The preschoolers stopped playing, growing anxious as they listened to the scuffle of rats, the garage dark except for the dim sunlight filtering through the murky windowpanes. The suffocating summer heat weighed on them until Amy panicked and punched out the garage door windows. She and Darlene fled the garage as Darlene's father yelled at them for breaking the glass. Amy ran home and her mom picked the shards from Amy's right knuckles before sending her outside to play.

A year later Amy walked home from a friend's house, passing by the cantankerous Siamese cat living two doors down. The cat lunged at Amy and wrapped its limbs around her leg, clawing and biting her so deeply, she had to use her other foot to kick off the cat. And at age twelve, as Amy played kickball in the street with friends, a temperamental English shepherd named Oliver charged across the street at her, sinking his teeth into her right calf.

Amy recounts, *"I had just seen the movie Jaws, and I can still see the dog's full set of teeth in my leg."*

No stitches for Amy and no accountability for Oliver's haywire attack although this wasn't his first attack in the neighborhood.

Not long after the dog bite, Amy tagged along with her mom and new stepdad to Lakewood Park for the fireworks show on July 4th. Amy grabbed her chance to enjoy the view of Lake Erie and the Cleveland skyline, climbing atop a chain link fence designed to keep spectators from venturing down to the waterfront. She reached the top and grabbed the metal crisscross pattern just as her foot slipped. The fence's vertical wires sliced her hand as she fell to the ground. Her stepdad drove her to the hospital in his orange Camero and let her wear his sunglasses as a doctor

stitched her up, the scar now an ever-present reminder of the fall, her first stitches, and her stepdad, a man who served as a loving, calm presence in her life.

Amy says, *"I enjoyed my childhood, as unconstrained as it was.... the days were gloriously long—full of play, catching lightning bugs in the front yard, bike riding with friends, cooking with my Nonna, delivering the newspaper with my brother on dark cold and snowy mornings."*

Amy grew up. She became a runner. She graduated from the University of Michigan and the University of Virginia, married, remarried, and raised three daughters. But she still carries the scars that remind her of a life before minivans and cell phones—a time when kids learned to fend for themselves, unsupervised and free.

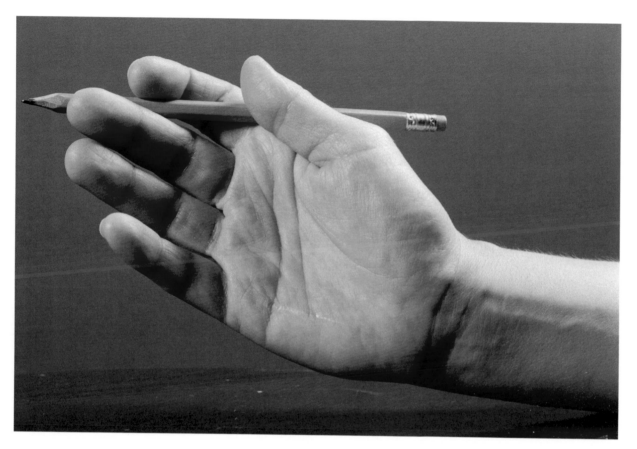

I enjoyed my childhood, as unconstrained as it was...

Amy Ciliberto Barrett

Omar Sedky

S t o r y   6

n early 2013, Omar spent three days trapped inside Yemen's Sana'a US Embassy after protests escalated outside the compound. He says, *"After escaping, I chose to make the most of my life."* Taking his lead from Matt Cutts's TED Talk, he began to try something new every day, capturing it with a daily photo. *"I'm passionate about being a better person. To better the world, we must better ourselves,"* says Omar.

Omar grew up in an eminent family in the Mohandeseen district of Giza, one of four cities within greater Cairo. Mohandeseen's architecture reflects the starkly contrasting worlds found within its walls. One half of the neighborhood expands in a half circle outward from Arab League Boulevard; the other half comprises a traditional design of Roman-style city blocks. Worlds jostle for space in the neighborhood. Foreign embassies sit around the corner from notorious red-light districts, millionaires employ migrant doormen on call around the clock, prominent Muslim mosques and Christian churches perch side by side—cordial but wary neighbors.

A philosophy that binds these holy houses is respect for one's body. Manmade creations such as tattoos are forbidden by Islamic conservatives. Some take physical purity a step further, claiming accidental marks on the body such as scars are a result of divine punishment. Omar says that although he doesn't encounter much negative reaction to his scars in the U.S., *"if I were in*

Egypt and belonged to a lower-class family, my scar would affect my social status and job prospects."

On the day Omar was born in a Cairo hospital, a nurse scarred his thigh. Her long ungloved fingernails ripped his skin so deeply she removed pigment. And at four years old, Omar returned to the hospital for surgery resulting in his second scar. The doctors removed an infected ingrown hair on his right temple, but the skin graft procedure to cover up the smaller surgical incision left a noticeable mark. When Omar was twelve, his mother offered him a second round of plastic surgery to remove the scar, but he said no. *"I like it now. It's part of who I am."*

In 2012, Omar was living in DC, working for the Department of Defense. Mid-July, he and friends traveled to Ocean City, Maryland for the weekend. They sat outside a hotel, drinking beer and chatting with a couple of girls they'd met that night when they were interrupted by the girl's brother. What started as angry words ended with Omar being pushed through a plate-glass window. The scars imprinted along his back taught him a lesson: to drink less and pay more attention to escalating situations. He concentrates now on pursuing his passions as a MBA student focusing on international markets, trade, and their social implications. Eventually he wants to run his own corporation and foundation.

He says, *"The corporation will be the moneymaker while the foundation will help save the world."*

Although in America Omar's opportunities remain unblemished by his scars, around the world scars on working-class bodies incur the sting of social stigma and diminishing job prospects. With so much opportunity now at his fingertips, Omar works to make the world a better place by first making himself into a better man.

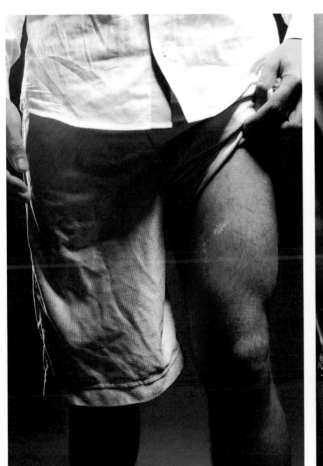 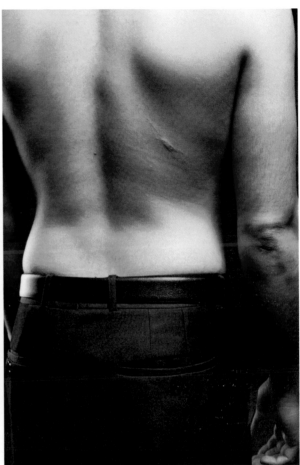

I'm passionate about being a better person.

Omar Sedky

Jared Osmond

ared took his first breath on a warm spring day.
The world waited for him, the hospital room abuzz
with his mother in labor, his father anxiously awaiting
his fourth child, the obstetrician close by, the nurse
with a watchful eye on the monitors, and extra medical
staff waiting on the sidelines—a precautionary measure
for Jared and his mother, Michelle. At his twenty-week
ultrasound, a grainy image revealed Jared suffered
from AVSD, a congenital heart defect. On the day he
was born, Michelle waited to hold her son as nurses
conducted tests, confirming Jared breathed easily on
his own. Michelle knew her son required open-heart
surgery to seal the left and right sides of his heart
but in those first moments together she thought of
nothing but her new baby, holding him close, sensing
his peaceful countenance in their first minutes together.

Four months later, Michelle carried Jared into the
Children's Hospital for surgery as his three older siblings
slept at home.

Before becoming a full-time mom, Michelle ranked as
a captain in the military. She trained with machine guns.
She drove armored personnel tanks. She spent weeks
in the wilderness for weapons training. But she faltered
the morning of Jared's surgery, struggling as she handed
her youngest over to the nurse, watching him disappear
through the swinging doors to pre-op.

So she sat. And waited. Four hours of anesthesia and life
support for Jared, four hours of heart repair and valve

reconstruction for Dr. Jonas and his team, and four long hours of forgettable chitchat between Michelle and Keith as they waited to see their son.

"You very quickly accept things when you have no other choice," says Michelle.

When surgery was over, they weren't allowed to see him. Only after Jared stabilized, his parents entered his room. He lay covered in tubes, a tiny figure on the hospital bed. Michelle leaned over her son whispering the words from his *Winnie the Pooh* book.as the nurse pulled tubes from his body.

"One happy butterfly dancing in the sky, two great big acorns to make an acorn pie."

Jared calmed to Michelle's voice, surprising the nurse as he lay quietly while she slid each tube, one by one from his body.

Last May, Jared celebrated his third birthday; a milestone he wouldn't have met without open heart surgery. Michelle drove her four children to Clemonjontri Park to celebrate—a vast colorful playground complete with a prancing horse carousel. After naptime and a walk around the block in his stroller, Jared sat in his sunny kitchen and ate his favorite dinner of basmati rice, green peas, and vegan chocolate cupcakes with chocolate icing.

Michelle calls Jared's scar his badge of honor— a badge he will carry throughout his life. Whenever he removes his shirt, his scar prominently displayed, he will remember the love and courage of his parents who made the first and most important decision of his life.

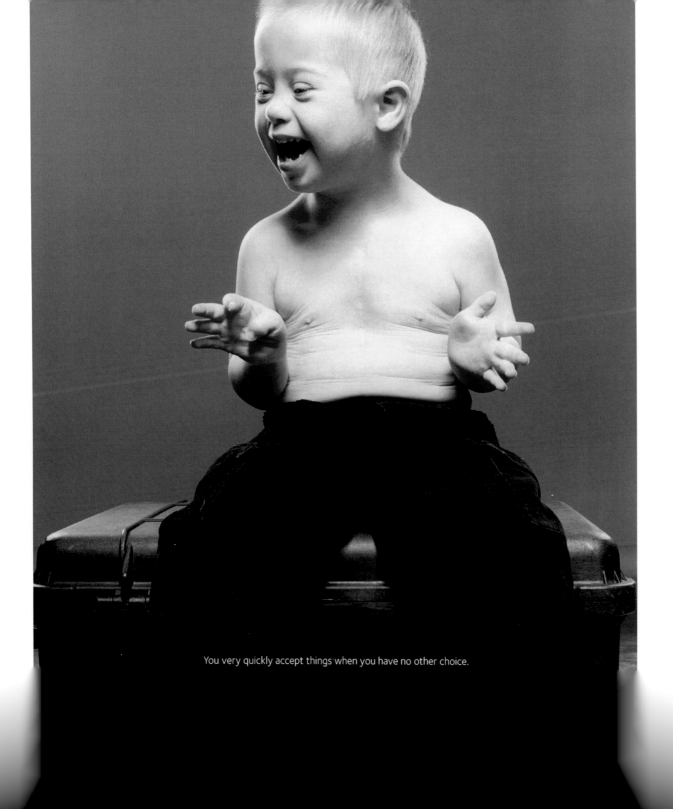

You very quickly accept things when you have no other choice.

Karen Lovelace

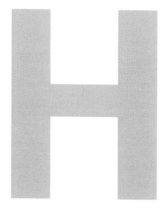igh up in the Rocky Mountains in Canada, Karen navigated the moguls alongside her travel buddies until her 350-pound friend slammed into her, falling on top of her, and obliterating the cartilage under her knee.

Arthritis haunted her after the arthroscopic surgery needed to repair her leg. One month of rehab allowed Karen back on her feet, but ten years later she underwent a chrome knee replacement to alleviate the long term damage, a surgery memorialized with a seven inch scar and a recovery period that left her feeling much older than her seventy three years.

Surgery stole her identity. After thirty seven years of running, which included fifteen marathons, twenty-six half marathons, and four triathlons, she was no longer a runner. And her doctor advised her it could take a year to get back into pre-surgery shape. But Karen ignored conventional advice and embraced the idea of remaking herself.

She told herself, *"Inside every runner, there is a walker."*

The first week she hobbled inside her house using a walker for support; the second week she limped outside to reach the neighbor's house. Two weeks later, the end of her street; two months later, three mile stretches. Two months after that, Karen walked five miles on the trails around her house in Reston, Virginia.

She says, *"I just told myself to take it past whatever my goal was yesterday."*

Now retired, Karen worked as an oncology nurse for fifty years in Washington, DC, witnessing the preciousness, the fleeting nature, and the impermanence of life. And she pursues new experiences at every turn. She recalls taking her four kids to the circus when she was a young mother. Her children teased her for being the only adult standing in line to ride the elephant. *"The people in line averaged about three years old, but I have this internal urgency to see and experience as much as I can until I can't."*

Hiking Romania, walking Spain, exploring Egypt, visiting Brazil—these vacation spots mean relaxation to many people, but they mean living life to the fullest to Karen. Her scar represents her outlook on life. Even when something slows her down, she never gives up on her passion for pursuing her next adventure.

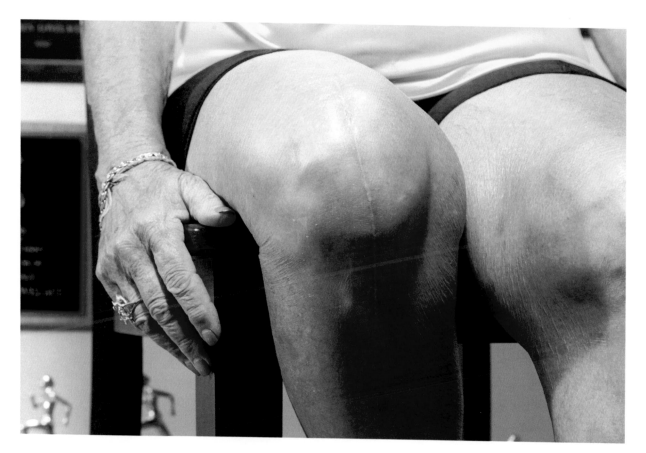

Inside every runner, there is a walker.

Karen Lovelace

Skylar Helms

I'll *never be a princess*," whispered four-year-old Skylar, sounding afraid for the first time since she was savagely attacked by a dog. Strapped in her car seat on the way to the grocery store, Skylar hung her head, crying as she rubbed the spiky red hair sprouting from her head. Her hair slow to grow because of the one hundred stitches she received after the attack. But Skylar has a knight in shining armor—her mom, Christine—who raises Skylar singlehandedly and continues to fight the accusations that claim her preschooler provoked the German shepherd into the aggressive attack.

Skylar and her mom attended an upscale dinner party on the evening of New Year's Day—a party hosted by her friend Dave's parents, prominent lawyers and residents of a community in northern Virginia. Skylar spent the evening close to her mom, pleased to discover a white German shepherd named Hoss lived in the house. Like most four-year-old girls, Skylar adores animals and lives with a bunny named Chubby Chunk and two dogs, Carlie and Charlie.

Later in the evening, Christine stood in the kitchen across from Dave, Skylar, and Hoss. Skylar rested her hand on the dog as if posing for a photograph. Without warning, Hoss attacked. The dog lunged sidewise across Skylar. He clamped his massive jaws onto the far side of her face, bit into her cheek, dragged her to the ground, and shook her back and forth as though weightless. When the dog momentarily released Skylar from his attack, Christine grabbed her daughter, rushed her to the car, and raced to the closest hospital.

Skylar wrapped her arms around her mom as Christine raced barefoot into the emergency room, forgetting her shoes at the party.

The nurses rushed to put Skylar onto a stretcher, calling for a doctor. The gashes on Skylar's face exposed raw tissue. Her skin ripped from her left eye to her left ear, her cheeks bitten down to her jaw-line, Skylar endured the panicked ride to the hospital without crying. Her silence broke as the nurse injected Skylar's face once, twice, and a third time in the head—a necessity to numb the area before the plastic surgeon stitched her face together.

Dave visited Christine the next morning and informed her his parents decided if the attack went to court, they would testify Skylar had provoked Hoss, in order to protect the dog. Christine called Dave's mother who hung up on her.

Their actions made her feel as if she lived *"in the same town as the devil,"* as she realized Hoss was the family's priority and not the safety of other people's children.

The state of Virginia summoned Dave's parents to court. Christine rearranged her and Skylar's plans for the first court date, but Dave's parents skipped their appearance. Christine rearranged her plans again, intent on testifying, refusing to allow Skylar to take the blame for the attack. With just one brother in Georgia and both parents deceased, she said, *"Skylar is the only family I've got, and I've got to defend her name."* She decided not to sue Dave's parents for the medical costs, instead paying for Skylar's recovery out of her own savings.

In late 2013, a jury decided Hoss should not receive his first warning in this case. The One Free Bite law in Virginia means Hoss receives his first warning only if he bites again. After this warning he can bite a third person before he is euthanized.

Unlike the German shepherd, Skylar lives with the consequences of her attack daily, her scars a permanent reminder. Skylar's dreams are interrupted by ferocious white tigers threatening to attack. But in her waking life, Skylar watches her mom—her protector, her advocate, her role model—initiating action with a Change.org petition to amend the One Free Bite law in Virginia. Watching her mom fight on her behalf, Skylar learns her fading scars are no match for the beauty of a resilient spirit.

I'll never be a princess.

Skylar Helms

Catherine Terranova

S t o r y   1 0

athy tortured herself until she accepted Jesus Christ into her heart. She sliced her upper arms, her inner thighs, body parts hidden by clothing. Her cutting a secretive and obsessive habit during her early teenage years, she sees the lingering scars as useful. Speaking about her scars, she quotes the Bible, *"What you call dirty, He calls clean. What you call broken, He calls useful. Where you are wounded, He longs to be invited and to call you healed."*

Finding healing in her faith, she is finally unashamed of the abuse she suffered as a child.

Cathy endured her first rape as a two-year-old, the incest continuing for six haunting years. She lived in fear. *"I was loved one minute and hated the next, I was hugged one moment, and slapped the next."* She was starved, beaten, and neglected—the target of her bully's anger. She entered elementary school with few friends, treated as the oddball: the girl with the wild, curly hair; the girl who cried too easily.

By third grade, she learned to smoke and steal and by middle school, a whirling dervish of hormones, she lost her footing altogether, uncertain how to handle her childhood trauma. Her emotions exploded. She hid behind her wild hair, colorful clothes, big laugh, shallow friendships, and mountains of schoolwork. Slicing open her skin in private brought her a sense of control and she didn't know how to stop.

"I hadn't learned that my body was a temple for a living God. Instead, it was a walking morgue for a girl who thought being dead was a better option," she says.

Cathy made a life-changing decision just after her sixteenth birthday. She accepted an invitation to a Christian retreat. She returned home and read one piece of Scripture a day, writing one thing she learned each day, taking her first steps to reconnect with life. On long solitary walks, she heard Christ speak to her.

The following year, she visited Passion—a Christian conference numbering 22,000 youth.

It was there she wandered into a prayer room and found a teenage girl crying on the floor. Fighting her instinct to leave, Cathy sat next to the girl and asked if they could pray together. The teenager confided in Cathy, telling her of abuse and abandonment by her father and finally disclosing her shame—she secretively cut herself. Cathy lifted her sleeve to reveal her own scars.

In that moment, she heard Christ say, *"Look at what I choose to do with you—despite all that I can accomplish without you."*

Three years later, just days before Cathy's wedding at which she wore a dress that exposed her scars, she received a text from the same girl thanking her for the time they spent together at *Passion*.

In 2011, formally diagnosed with chronic post traumatic stress disorder, Cathy started a regiment of regular therapy and medication. Open with her brokenness, she says *"I'm not okay. I haven't been for a long time, but that's okay."*

Cathy continues to learn how to confront her pain with God's help. Her battle with depression continues, but after years of engaging in self-destructive actions, she is true to God. She understands God won't give her a boat to travel in through life. Rather, He will stand next to her in the water, through the storms and in the calm. And through this understanding, she finally knows unconditional love.

I'm not okay. I haven't been for
a long time, but that's okay.

*Catherine
Terranora*

Amy Tippins

Leave it to a Southern belle. Amy uses her classic looks, her southern charm, and old fashioned stubbornness to abolish outdated notions of beauty. She wears thirty inches of scars across her stomach, thigh, and ankle and she carries decades of emotional scars—scars underscoring her remarkable success. Her most recent triumph is *RockScar Designs*—a modern trend-setting clothing company. But each success rose only after months—sometimes years—of quiet panic, dark clouds of uncertainty and loneliness obscuring Amy's way. Speaking about heartbreaking news she received in 2013, she says, *"I spent days in bed. I didn't eat. I didn't get dressed. I did nothing but lie in my bed."* Yet Amy chose to rise from the ashes, reinventing herself and redefining her goals once again.

Her largest scar, shown in the picture, resulted from a grueling sixteen-hour surgery when she was sixteen years old and days away from death—an end to a four-year struggle with a mystifying disease that changed her life forever.

Amy's life proved unremarkable until she turned twelve years old. Growing up in Gwinnet County, she lived with her two parents, not yet divorced, and an older brother she idolized. Amy attended church, made friends easily at school, and excelled at basketball and swimming.

But her world changed on a church trip to Clearwater, Florida. It was there she noticed little blisters on her ankles. Over the next few months, the blisters crept up Amy's legs, arms, and chest, and into her hairline, developing into deep ulcers. The onset of 103-degree fevers left her bedridden. She remembers, *"No one could figure out what was wrong with me. I had practically every medical test except for a spinal tap. They even tested me for HIV although I never had exposure to it. I was tested for Lupus and Hepatitis. I became jaundice. And I started going through a lot of pain lying on the floor for thirty minutes at a time feeling like a hot knife was slicing open my side."*

Insomnia kept her up for days until she collapsed. Confused thoughts wove through her daily interactions. She says, *"I could look at you and know your name but not have a clue who you were."*

Amy found herself in countless doctors' offices over the next few years. One physician suggested there was nothing physically wrong with her; her symptoms simply a method to pull attention away from her older athletic brother.

Amy's life at school degraded. Kids bullied her as she withdrew from her friends. Her swim coach kicked her out of most practices, accusing her of laziness and not living up to her talent. That year another medical specialist decided to do a double biopsy after discovering a shadow on a scan. Both biopsy needles missed tissue crucial to solving the mystery and doctors chalked up the shadow to a smudge on the machine.

During junior year, doctors quarantined Amy. In an isolated room at the hospital, her fevers lasted weeks. The nurses pushed antibiotics and food through a

window. A few weeks before Christmas, Amy met a liver specialist and he sent her for a CT scan. The results were startling. The specialist sat Amy down and told her she needed a liver transplant immediately. The blisters she discovered years beforehand signaled the first sign of liver failure. The pain of hot knives in her side was tumors rupturing inside her liver. Her confusion and insomnia were symptomatic of her brain malfunctioning from toxins her liver ceased to remove from her blood.

The name Amy Tippins was added to the national transplant list in January. Amy Tippins was removed from the list three weeks later as her surgeon vacationed. That week, she missed her first transplant opportunity. The following week, on Valentine's Day, her doctor informed her she had a week to live. As most sixteen-year-olds prepared for Valentine dates, Amy wrote her goodbyes to her parents. That afternoon, her donor died from a stroke.

Three days later Amy got the call.

The transplant surgery fraught with unexpected discoveries, surgeons removed half her diaphragm due to extensive scar tissue. Her liver was riddled with two dozen tumors, the largest measuring the size of a football. *"I should have been dead months earlier. If the tumors had been cancerous, they would have just sewn me up and sent me home to die,"* she recounts.

Amy recovered quickly but her battle wasn't over. She reeled at the eighteen-inch scar on her stomach. Already battling with self acceptance and body image issues, she fixated on how ugly her scars were and *"how*

I should have been dead months earlier.

A m y   T i p p i n s

no man will ever want me because I'm not perfect."
But by next summer she taught herself to embrace her
scar, wearing a bikini at the local pool, pushing herself to
make her scar a part of her identity.

Amy spent her twenties as a successful sales director,
proving her business acumen, before the economy
and her life crashed around her feet. Unemployed and
unable to walk for three months due to ankle surgery,
she took time to figure out her next move. *"I decided
I wanted to do something fun with clothing. I'm still
working out my emotional scars from my high school
years and I knew I wanted to do something about
transplantation."*

RockScar Designs jumped on the scene in 2010. Amy
fashions clothing dedicated to celebrating scars. She
says her company encourages people to view their
scars as a source of strength, of *"being a person of
character in life's most difficult moments . . . using life
struggles as stepping stones to greatness."*

In 2013, Amy's world collapsed again. Her heart broke
as her doctor explained she had a non-detectable egg
count—which means conceiving a child is slim to none.
She explains, *"The best theory my doctor has is I had
a hormone imbalance once I hit puberty. My body just
went nuts and whatever caused my tumors cooked my
ovaries."*

But she lives her message. She mourned her loss.
She wiped her tears. And now she divides her time
between *RockScar Designs* and finding a baby of her
own, jumping adoption hurdles and using this newest
experience as a stepping stone to her next great
adventure of becoming a mother.

Philip Nuar

hirty-three-year-old Philip dresses for success—dress shirts, pressed jeans, and colorful awareness bracelets that relay his young, hopeful attitude. Always on his A-game, Philip's positive attitude encourages him to keep looking for his next career choice, his next girlfriend, his next overseas adventure.

He takes meticulous care of his hair, traveling seventy-five miles every six weeks for his haircut. Four tumors in his brain took away his ability to drive so he asks around until a friend agrees to the four-hour round trip to and from the Johns Hopkins Hospital hair salon. The owner of the salon, a sixty-year-old brain cancer survivor, is the only stylist he knows that cuts his hair without poking the sensitive parts of his head—a side effect of numerous brain surgeries and, as he says, *"more radiation and chemotherapy than is safe for any human being."*

As a preschooler, Philip would often visit a petting zoo close to his house in Newfield, New Jersey, racing alongside his brothers and sisters toward the barn animals. One day, as his siblings ran ahead, he sat down, uninterested in feeding the goats, complaining to his mom of another headache. His mother realized something was wrong and scheduled a doctor's visit for Philip.

After a scan, doctors discovered Philip's headaches were caused by a highly malignant primary brain tumor. The prognosis: at four years old, he had just six months to live.

Philip has few memories of that time, but he will never forget screaming for his mother as he was wheeled toward the operating room for his first brain surgery. Over the next four months, Philip traveled between his house and the hospital for chemotherapy and radiation treatments in an attempt to kill what was left of the tumor.

Philip's first scar appeared after doctors inserted a catheter in his chest during those treatments. The volume of needles required to draw blood to monitor the effects of chemotherapy and radiation scared Philip. He cried, kicked, and wrestled away from the nurses as they injected him, eventually requiring six adults to hold him down. The catheter inserted under his collarbone alleviated the pain and fear of Philip's continuing blood tests and injections. A later surgery removed the catheter, leaving a permanent scar on his chest—a badge of the first operation of many Philip would survive over the next three decades.

Philip acquired the scar on his abdomen shown in the accompanying photograph in ninth grade. At thirteen, he traveled around New Jersey with his swim team. One day at practice he bumped into a pool deck. A massive bump appeared later that week, the protrusion growing larger and darker. A biopsy revealed Philip's second round with cancer. This time it was skin cancer. Surgery removed the cancer, along with his ability to swim and play soccer.

Unable to play the sports he loved, Philip focused on another passion: traveling. He traveled sometimes with family, sometimes with friends, sometimes alone. He explored South America, Europe, and many parts of the US. His wanderlust eventually led him to Mexico,

then to Austria as a university student. While in Austria, Philip studied international relations during the week, traveling to Spain and Italy on the weekends, and ignoring the new tennis-ball size growth in his throat. When he returned to the U.S at Christmas, his doctor informed him the lump was thyroid cancer; he required two surgeries to remove the cancer and his thyroid gland.

At twenty-five years old, Philip learned about the four new tumors in his brain. For the past eight years a MRI every four months pronounces the tumors stagnant, but each year Philip undergoes surgery and radiation to maximize his odds of survival. Philip's attitude toward doctors and prognosis is defiant.

"I'm still alive because I don't listen to the doctors anymore. And I stay busy," he says.

Philip volunteers with cancer survivors and the Knights of Columbus. He runs 5Ks for cancer research, rides horseback, zip-lines, plays mini-golf, and continues to travel the world.

Although he wants to be in a relationship, he is certain he will remain childless—out of love for the children he will never hold. He is afraid that he might pass on a genetic predisposition to cancer. *"I wouldn't wish this life on anyone,"* says Philip.

But each day, as he steps out in the world, Philip transforms his struggle with cancer into a journey of faith and exploration, always planning for his future.

Today the sun shines on Philip. Today he chooses his own adventure. Today he chooses to fight the cancer inside.

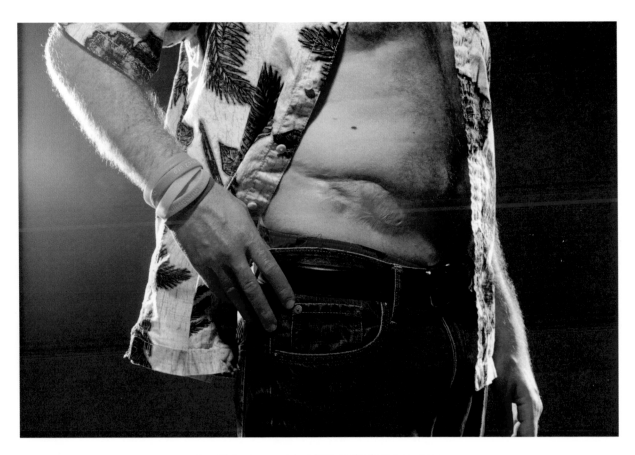

I'm still alive because I don't listen to the doctors anymore.

Philip Nuar

Thank you for reading.

We hope *Who I am: American Scar Stories* inspired and entertained you.

If you enjoyed this book, we would love to read your positive review at *www.goodreads.com* and your national Amazon site at *www.amazon.com*, *www.amazon.ca*, or *www.amazon.uk*

Please subscribe to *www.jennycutlerlopez.com* if you are interested in receiving:
- Updates on the people featured in this book
- Inspirational nonfiction short stories
- Subscriber giveaways
- Information on future books by Jenny
- Useful tips on writing and publishing nonfiction

To leave feedback or contact the author, please email Jenny at *jennycutlerlopez@gmail.com*

I'd like to extend my deepest gratitude and heartfelt thanks to the people who provided support and assistance to allow me to create this book.

· Michelle Osmond for taking care of my children and her daily encouragement as I conducted interviews
· Valerie Geary and Brenton Newell for feedback and tips on the publishing process and book proposal
· Brandy King, Terri Anderson, and Miki Hsu Leavey as first readers
· Tim Acuna for his time, his faith, and his photographic expertise
· Holly J. Schumacher for her professionalism and photographic expertise
· C.S. Lakin for professionally editing the text
· Timothy Jones for the incredible interior and cover design
· Dave Mezzapelle for his support and thoughtful foreword
· Each person featured in this book along with the people who support and encourage them to tell their story. Courtney Ott, Jane and Greg Ott, Amy Tippins, BethAnn Telford, Dr. Bob Latin, Philip Nuar, Skylar Helms, Christine Foster, Jose Rios, Krystian Leonard, Karime Leonard, Cathy Terranova and Doug Terranova, Omar Sedky, Jared Osmond, Michelle and Keith Osmond, Amy Ciliberto Barrett, Karen Lovelace and Mari Acuna for putting me in touch with Courtney Ott.
· And my most heartfelt love and thanks to the man with whom I share my life as well the idea for this book: Jacques G. Lopez. His support and encouragement never cease to transform my ideas into reality

Contacts:

Jenny Cutler Lopez *www.jennycutlerlopez.com*
Tim Acuna *www.acunastudios.com*
Holly J. Schumacher *www.hollyjimages.com*
Timothy Jones *timothy_jones5@yahoo.ca*
Brandy King *www.knowledge-linking.com*
Terri Anderson *andersoncommunications.cl*
Dave Mezzapelle *www.contagiousoptimism.com*
C.S. Lakin *www.livewritethrive.com*

Featured in the book:

Krystian Leonard *www.shiningscars.org*
BethAnn Telford *www.teambt.org*
Cathy Terranova *www.cathyterranova.wordpress.com*
Amy Tippins *www.rockscardesigns.com*

CPSIA information can be obtained
at www.ICGtesting.com
Printed in the USA
BVXC01n1135190514
353694BV00002B/3

9 780996 060400